THE
NEW FATHER
SURVIVAL GUIDE

T H E
NEW FATHER
S U R V I V A L   G U I D E
LARRY SNYDAL · CARL JONES

Illustrated by
Richard Blaine

1987 Franklin Watts
New York   Toronto

To Jeff

Good luck

Larry Snydal

Library of Congress Cataloging-in-Publication Data

Snydal, Larry.
The new father survival guide.

Bibliography: p.
1. Fathers—United States.   2. Father and child—
United States.   I. Jones, Carl.   II. Title.
HQ756.S548   1987   306.8'742   87-14723
ISBN 0-531-15063-1

TABLE OF
CONTENTS

FOREWORD
1

INTRODUCTION
5

THE POSTPARTUM PERIOD
9

THE FIRST HOUR
11

HOMECOMING
17

HER CHANGING BODY
21

PATERNITY LEAVE
25

WHAT'S A DAD TO DO?
29

GETTING HOUSEHOLD HELP
33

MEETING YOUR OWN NEEDS
37

ADJUSTMENTS
41

BABY BLUES
47

GETTING TO KNOW YOU
53

THE LAYETTE
59

THE GREAT ESCAPE
63

TWIST AND SHOUT
67

THE NURSE FATHER
73

BOTTLEFEEDING
79

LOVEMAKING
81

THE ROCK OF GIBRALTAR
85

THE CESARIAN FATHER
91

FOOD FOR THOUGHT: RECIPES
97

SUPPORT GROUPS
133

SELECTED READING LIST
135

T H E
NEW FATHER
SURVIVAL GUIDE

© BLAINE 1984

FOREWORD

I still remember how over-whelmed I felt when I first came home with my wife, Claudia, and our newborn baby, Jonathan. It was hard to believe I was really a father. Two weeks later I was still overwhelmed, especially when our son cried and was unresponsive to our best efforts to calm him. How I wish I had this book when my first child was born! It should be in the hands of every expectant and new father.

As a psychiatrist who specializes in working with families, I'm often struck by how few childbirth profes-sionals recognize or support the new father's needs. Most books—like most support groups—are focused on the mother-infant dyad. Fathers are frequently left out. Though today's father is expected to participate during

1

labor, society acts as if he is not supposed to show his feelings, his anxieties, his needs. The father who does show his feelings is likely to hear something like: "What are you complaining about? You didn't go through anything. Your wife is the one who had the baby."

That's why this book is such a gem.

Written in a concise, down-to-earth, humorous yet highly informative style, this book fills a long-unmet need for new parents. It offers every man the support, reassurance, and basic information he needs, while showing fathers how to be an integral, participating member of the new family from the very beginning. In simple terms it addresses all the common medical issues about which new fathers ask questions. It tells the father what he needs to know about the newborn baby and about that most energy-draining subject of all—the baby's crying.

The father's attitude and support can actually spell the difference between breastfeeding success and failure, the authors point out. As never before, this book shows precisely how the father can support his partner's breastfeeding and diminish his own sense of isolation.

And this handbook answers the very basic questions about sexual relations—questions most men share but are often too embarrassed to discuss.

To my mind, including simple recipes at the end of the book, as Carl Jones and Larry Snydal have done, is a wonderful idea for the new dad who wants to help his partner with the cooking during the chaotic postpartum period. Dad's contribution in this and other practical household areas should not be overlooked. It means so much to his recovering partner.

From my own professional experience, I can say that the father's involvement with his child and his support of his partner during the postpartum period benefits the marriage relationship tremendously. The father who actively participates during those early weeks and months after a baby is born almost invariably feels better about himself and makes a smoother transition to his new lifelong role. By showing the new father how to help the mother as he builds a special relationship with his child, this little handbook benefits the entire family.

No man will regret following the steps this book outlines. It will give him some very special moments to treasure.

Martin Greenberg, M.D., author of
The Birth of a Father and co-author
of *Experts Advise Parents*

INTRODUCTION

The baby's born. The focal point belongs to photography again, and controlled breathing to yoga. The last brow has been mopped, labor is over. *Mind Over Labor* and Lamaze fade into the background like the titles of grade-B films. It's time to throw out all the handouts from the childbirth class, time to forget those Tuesday evenings on the floor with five other pregnant couples, time to move all the books about pregnancy to the back bedroom. Time to send the cards and make the telephone calls. Everything is back to normal.

Wait a minute! The little bundle that lay so long in its human wrapping, making your mate nauseous in the A.M. and your lovemaking innovative, is still around. But now it's unwrapped. Things are not back to normal.

We'll get a routine . . . Things
will even out . . . Honest

What you need now is an extended family of relations *and* friends. And nerves of steel and muscles of iron. And the patience of Job. Because things will *never* be back to normal.

New dads treat their situation in all kinds of ways. The suggestions in this book will help you to find your own style and stick with it. If you're comfortable with cooking, now's the time for it. If you don't mind a little housework, help out. If your bent is cuddling, make friends with the new family member. Maybe you held the newborn, and maybe you placed him on Mama's stomach. Don't stop there—stay involved. The more you do, the more you'll feel like a father. And that's important.

Sometimes men feel it's not masculine to cuddle and play with a baby. But there's nothing exclusively feminine about cuddling and loving. Ask your wife. Dads have been raising children as long as moms have.

Maybe your work takes you away from home for long hours or even for days at a time. Think quality. Work at being a father when you're home. It takes money to raise a family—nobody argues with that. But keep your priorities straight. Being a good father is the biggest job any man will ever have.

THE POSTPARTUM PERIOD

The *postpartum* period (from the Latin *post*, "after," and *partum*, "bearing") is the first six weeks following birth. A lot can and does happen during this life-transforming time. The mother's body returns to its nonpregnant condition. Your lives change dramatically, irreversibly. The transition to new motherhood and new fatherhood is often rocky. This is the time to remember that the father's role doesn't end with giving support during labor. In fact, your role is just beginning.

The practical advice in the pages ahead is offered to help you and your partner make these six weeks (and beyond) incredibly rewarding and fulfilling.

THE FIRST HOUR

In the moments after birth you will doubtless be excited, ecstatic, and flooded with pride and joy. You will also probably be thoroughly exhausted. Your mate has been through a lot—and so have you. It's not easy to give support through the long hours of labor. Those hours of walking with your partner, of encouraging her with soothing words, of rubbing her back all take their toll on you, too.

But the moment when the baby comes—no book or film can prepare you for that! The struggle is finally over. You are now Dad.

THE BABY

The baby may have a creamy white substance called *vernix caseosa* here and there on the skin, especially

11

around the armpits and groin. This protected the baby's delicate skin while he was in his watery uterine home. Rather than wipe it away, let it remain right where it is. Take a small bit of the vernix between your fingers— you will find it a luxurious-feeling skin cream. In the past some fathers rubbed vernix onto the woodwork of their prize rifles. Whatever you do with it, don't throw it away!

There may be a bit of blood, too, especially if the mother tore. It wipes right off.

If your baby's head looks like that of an alien from outer space, don't worry. Newborns' heads often look a bit squashed in on one side, or pointed. This is perfectly normal. It will shape up in a day or two. Nature designed the newborn's soft skull to mold to the birth outlet during labor.

The baby may also appear a little bluish at first. However, he or she will "pink up" in five minutes or so. The hands and feet may take as long as a day.

SPENDING THE FIRST HOUR TOGETHER

Your first hours with your newborn will probably be one of the most dramatic experiences of your entire fatherhood.

Studies have shown that the first hour following birth is a particularly sensitive time for both parents and babies. The baby, if born after an undrugged labor, is highly alert. The parents are especially sensitive, ready to explore and "take in" their new child.

Psychiatrist Martin Greenberg, author of *The Birth of a Father*, refers to the father's preoccupation with his newborn as *engrossment*. According to Dr. Greenberg, engrossment includes an intense visual and tactile awareness of the baby, as well as a strong attraction to the infant. The initial engrossment is usually characterized by feelings of exhilaration and elation.

It is extremely important that you and your partner spend the first hour with your baby without being interrupted—except, of course, for the all-important phone calls. Separation from the baby during the hours immediately following birth can interrupt the parent-infant bonding (attachment) process. This is an extremely delicate phase of your relationship with your newborn; and separation may cause serious postpartum problems for your mate. In fact, as pointed out in Carl Jones's *After the Baby Is Born,* maternal-infant separation during the first hour after birth is the number-one cause of postpartum blues. There will be plenty of times in the weeks and months that follow when you will want nothing more than to be separated from your crying baby for a spell. However, the first hour is a time to remain together.

Following are the basics to make the most of the first hour after birth:

Cut the umbilical cord. Some fathers want to do this themselves. It doesn't hurt either the mother or the baby. Since the umbilical cord is going to have to be cut one of these days, you might as well be the one to do it.

Cutting the cord can be a symbolic gesture you'll always remember—like placing the ring on the bride's finger.

The procedure is simple. Your caregiver* will clamp the cord in two places; simply snip it with a pair of scissors between the clamps.

Be sure to wait until the cord stops pulsing and the blood stops flowing through it, so the baby can get the nutrients from the placenta for an added boost at life's dramatic beginning.

Hold the baby skin to your skin. Remove your shirt. Don't feel embarrassed about this. Many fathers today remove their shirts after hospital births as well as home births to establish that wonderful skin-to-skin contact with their child. Besides, the mother has removed enough of her clothes to give birth. You can certainly take off your shirt!

Noodleneck needs a hand behind the head and one under his body when you pick him up. Bring him right up to your shoulder or the crook of your arm. Both positions feel perfectly natural immediately, and you won't hurt him. He's small but not fragile. Just remember, support the head and neck now when he's small. You'll be supporting the rest of him for some time to come.

A blanket over any exposed parts of the baby and a cap on her head will provide sufficient warmth.

Newborn babies don't smell like anything else. They have a nice, fresh, sweet scent. Have you noticed it?

* The word *caregiver* is used throughout this book to refer to anyone who provides health care to a woman during pregnancy, labor, and the postpartum period. The caregiver may be a midwife, obstetrician, family practitioner, naturopath, chiropractor, or the like.

Take a look at those fingernails. Small but complete. Amazing, aren't they?

Experience eye contact. This is one of the high points following birth. For some fathers it is as overwhelming as witnessing the birth itself.

Be sure the room is dimly lit; newborns' eyes are extremely sensitive. (Yours would be, too, if you had just spent nine months underwater in the dark.) In a dimly lit room, the baby can see best a few inches in front of her face—in fact, at precisely the distance to the mother's head as she breastfeeds. The newborn's eyes will open wide and take in her first sight of her new dad. That memory—before words, before thoughts—will stay with her for the rest of her life.

Avoid interruptions. Unless there is a genuine complication requiring immediate pediatric attention, postpone all medical procedures—including weighing and measuring the baby—until after the first hour following birth. Postpone also the use of prophylactic eyedrops (which prevent infection). These temporarily sting the baby's eyes and blur the vision, preventing the initial eye-to-eye contact.

Don't forget to let your mate have some time with the baby, too. After all, she worked hard enough for it. She should begin breastfeeding as soon as possible. The baby needs the antibodies in the yellowish premilk substance *colostrum* to prevent a host of diseases. Nursing immediately after birth is also important for the mother. When the baby nurses, the hormone oxytocin is released, causing the uterus to contract. This facilitates the delivery of the placenta and later causes the uterus to clamp down over exposed blood vessels to prevent postpartum hemorrhage.

Even if you have planned on bottlefeeding, it is wise to give the baby the breast during the first hour following birth.

Finally, if you haven't done so already, kiss your partner. Congratulate each other. The hard part is over. Only eighteen or so years to go.

Don't feel guilty if you cannot spend the first hour with your baby. Although this is a sensitive time and should be spent together if at all possible, bonding is not an instant glue phenomenon like epoxy (whose label also claims skin-to-skin bonding if you should get the glue on your fingers). You can make up for lost time later.

If there is a serious medical problem and the baby must be taken to an intensive care unit (ICU) for immediate pediatric care, you and your mate can accompany the baby. If your mate is being stitched as a result of tearing, you can go to the ICU and later share with her the infant's first actions.

HOMECOMING

The first day in a new life! After watching and wondering during the pregnancy, after hours of panting and pushing, the reward is here. A tiny reward in one way—look at the fingers! In another way, not tiny at all—how did he ever fit inside? But here he is, and it's the beginning of a new life for all three of you.

How different your wife looks! Tired—tired to the bone—but elated and glowing. You've shared things before but never this—the first day in the life of a new family.

IN THE HOSPITAL OR CHILDBEARING CENTER

Remain with your mate throughout her postpartum stay, if possible. In some hospitals fathers can room-in

with the new family for twenty-four hours, which is the way it should be. If this arrangement is not possible at the facility where you gave birth, plan to visit your partner often.

Get involved with baby care. Although there are nurses who do this expertly, it is important for both parents to get familiar with caring for their own baby as early as possible. That way you will feel less awkward later.

Don't hesitate to ask questions. In addition, many birthing facilities have films and short classes for new parents about breastfeeding, diapering, bathing the baby, and so forth.

If you and your partner give birth in the hospital, consider early discharge (within twenty-four hours). At childbearing centers new mothers generally leave within twelve hours after birth. Some hospitals are beginning to encourage this, too. However, many do not; it is really up to the mother when she will leave. If in doubt about medical complications, check with the caregiver.

Home is the best place for an unfolding family during this very sensitive time. Imagine spending your honeymoon in the hospital! The first days with your new baby are a similarly special time. Familiar surroundings will make the life-altering transition smoother.

Many new parents remain in hospitals because they believe that there they will be able to get much-needed rest. We all know the mother needs to take it easy during the first days after birth. However, hospitals are not very restful places, especially for new families. They are for ill people—not for healthy babies and mothers (to say nothing of dads, who often feel like visitors there rather than integral parts of the family). If it's rest and relaxation you want, you'd be better off in a motel or resort. Besides, it's cheaper.

Early discharge may also help you avoid postpartum blues. The new mother wants to be back in her nest, and you don't want to come back to an empty house. Not now, when you've just been busy filling it. It's nice to have close relatives or a close friend awaiting your arrival—perhaps with a home-cooked meal if you can arrange it. Plan a celebration dinner, even if it's a takeout. But avoid a big party.

If you've had a home birth, you're already home. Those walls that monthly payments keep between you and the rest of us have never felt more secure. Unlike being in many hospitals, there'll be no question of separation—your new family is together right from the start.

Have your caregiver's telephone number handy if there are questions or problems once you are at home.

HER CHANGING BODY

The changes in a new mother's body are utterly amazing. Giving birth is probably the only time in your partner's life when she lost at least ten pounds in a single day (the combined weight of baby, placenta, and amniotic fluid). She will continue to lose weight as her body changes back to its former condition.

The belly does shrink—but don't expect that after six weeks it will look just like it did before she was pregnant. Her rippling water-bed belly might take several months to resume its previous shape. Exercise and common-sense nutrition will help.

Your partner shouldn't begin a reducing diet while she is nursing. Her body needs extra calories, protein, nutrients, and fluids to produce nature's perfectly designed, prepackaged baby food.

The uterus shrinks like a slowly deflating balloon. By about the tenth postpartum day, you can no longer feel the uterus above the pubic bone. As it shrinks, your partner will have a discharge called *lochia*. This consists of blood, vaginal secretions, and material from the uterine walls that nourished the baby and kept it secure.

Lochia starts off like a heavy menstrual flow, then gradually tapers off. For the first three days it is red. During this time lochia may be occasionally expelled in the form of clots, so if you see something that looks like a small piece of liver, don't panic. After the third day, the discharge becomes pink or brown and is a bit watery. Finally, about ten days after birth, lochia becomes almost colorless or yellowish.

Your partner may notice more lochia after getting up from a lying position. This is a result of pooling in the vagina. Also, lochia sometimes becomes more reddish after physical activity. This is a sign that she should be taking it easy.

Lochia has a fleshy odor (like menstrual blood but sometimes a little stronger), but it should not be offensive. A strong, foul odor may indicate an infection and should be referred to the caregiver. Heavy, bright red bleeding should be reported to the caregiver without delay.

Regular menstrual periods will start up again in about eight weeks in the nonnursing mother and from two to eighteen months (usually within five or six) in the nursing mother.

Your partner will probably feel a lot more tired than either of you imagined. Having a baby is hard work—to say nothing of what comes afterward.

Rest, relaxation, fresh air, and you are the best aids to her rapid recovery. Make sure she gets plenty of rest. Sound impossible? Help out with some of her household duties, and encourage her to take a nap now and then when the baby is sleeping. If you are at home the first week after birth, it will be a lot easier. You, your partner, and your baby will have a much easier time adjusting.

She is bound to be uncomfortable now and then, especially during the first few days after birth. Sore bottom. Sore breasts. Fatigue. You can help her feel more comfortable. See *After the Baby Is Born* for easy ways to relieve the discomforts.

PATERNITY LEAVE

Have you thought about taking a paternity leave? If so, be sure to take off the first week after birth. Although you may not be paid for the time you take off, the benefits of a week's paternity leave will more than outweigh the financial loss.

Paternity leave will give you a chance to bond with your infant. Being with the baby will further your fathering, and it will bring out strong paternal feelings during a time when everyone's emotions are close to the surface.

Also, your mate needs you. Studies have shown that the father's involvement during and after birth reduces postbirth difficulties for the entire family. Regardless of how many people your partner may have helping her, no one can replace you. Even if you don't do all the

25

©BLAINE'84

cooking and cleaning, just be at home with her—it will make a world of difference. Many mothers recall how much they depended on their mates during that first week after birth.

Even if you take only a few days off, your presence and your help at home will show your commitment to your family and your welcome to its new member.

You might want to consider paternity leave again later on. In some countries (Norway and Sweden) this is quite usual. People in those countries realize that when young children are raised with a maximum of attention, they require less attention later on. There are always exceptions; no statistics tell all the truth. But if you can wangle a week or two now, when the baby is young, chances are you won't even remember the financial hardship in ten years. You *will* remember the joy and exhilaration you experienced during your child's infancy. Your child will remember it, too. This kind of leave may sound impossible to you—think of all the bills and your new obligations! But sit down seriously sometime and consider it. Are there ways around financial deadlines? Resources you haven't plumbed yet?

As Dr. David Stewart, executive director of the National Association for Parents and Professionals for Safe Alternatives in Childbirth (NAPSAC), points out, "Fatherhood is the ultimate of manhood. Being a father is the one thing that only a man can do. Take pride in it and apologize to no one for giving your time and first consideration to your family, sometimes putting your job second."*

* David Stewart, "Father to Father on Breastfeeding," Info. Sheet No. 128, La Leche League International, Franklin Park, IL 60131, 1977.

WHAT'S A
DAD TO DO?

Dad's role after birth is just as important as Dad's role during birth.

Your presence in the hospital, childbearing center, or home strengthens the family bond, reduces the likelihood of baby blues, and makes the transition to parenthood immeasurably easier all around. And once you are back home, there are also a number of things you can do to benefit your new family.

Get to know your baby. Don't wait until the kid is old enough to play ball to begin relating to her. Hold the baby. She'll fit on your shoulder or on your lap or in the crook of your arm. Kind of cute, isn't she?

Change diapers; change the baby's clothes. Give her a bath. Don't worry if you feel a little awkward at first. All new fathers do.

Take charge of the housekeeping. Some people suggest letting the housework go. That's fine for some. However, for others there's nothing more depressing than an inch of dust. Besides, the first few days with the baby are special. You and your partner deserve to have everything looking its best.

Some jobs can be ignored. The lawn doesn't have to be mowed. The car doesn't have to be washed. But you can't ignore food (including food for Kitty and Rover) and laundry. Washing machines and dryers are made to be run by amateurs. Rooms can be dusted and vacuumed by males just as well as they can by females.

Has your partner always done the cooking? Why don't you give it a try? There are a lot of easy casseroles you can make with a can opener. Anyone can fry a hamburger or scramble a couple of eggs. Use the recipes in the back of this book for other dishes.

Consider fast food. Try Chinese for nutritious and usually inexpensive meals. A deli sandwich? Some cities have gourmet take-out restaurants. They're not cheap, but this would certainly be good for a celebration.

Hiring someone to cook a few nights a week is expensive. However, you may be able to get friends and relatives to help with the meals. One of the best postpartum gifts friends and relatives can offer is a home-cooked meal. Ask for a casserole instead of one more receiving blanket.

Who does the shopping? Where does all that food come from? Find out. Plan menus and check your supplies before you make a shopping list. Otherwise you'll drive yourself crazy with extra trips and the discovery that you have twenty-three boxes of cornstarch.

Try to strike a happy balance. If you are doing the housework yourself, be sure you don't get so caught up in it that you forget to spend time with your mate and baby.

And remember, it doesn't have to be permanent. There'll be more time and less strain later.

Mother the new mother. Give soft words, touches, and extra attention. New mothers are especially sensitive and vulnerable. Your mate will want to know that she is still loved. This is a time for understanding and patience.

During the first weeks after birth, little things count. Bring home a gift. Even if it's just a bunch of daisies, it will probably be immensely appreciated.

Bear in mind that it's not how much you do that counts but your presence at home—and your love.

GETTING HOUSEHOLD HELP

Arrange for help around the house. Most new parents need assistance during the first few days and weeks. Grandparents, other relatives, and friends traditionally aid a new family by preparing home-cooked meals and doing housekeeping as well as by enjoying the baby during the initial days.

It can be great if Mother or Mother-in-Law is there to help. Grandma can answer all kinds of questions that a new mom or dad may not even know to ask. But don't forget you're a parent now, too. Don't let Grandma hog the baby. Hug, not hog—remind her. If she's the helpful sort, ask her to teach you how to do unfamiliar chores. She'll feel good, and you'll learn something. (If you don't know how to change a diaper, watch. There's a handy skill.)

Yeah, well, the same as yesterday but
with more onions and hold the anchovies.

Don't refuse offers of help. The postpartum period is no time to try to do everything yourself. You will probably need all the help you can get.

One of the best postpartum gifts friends or relatives can offer is household help. If you don't feel too odd about it, let people know that. Many people don't realize that this often means a lot more than another baby gift. Besides, at this time the parents need a gift more than the baby does.

If you don't have relatives or friends living nearby to help out with the housekeeping, rent a helper: that friendly high-schooler. Or consider hiring a postpartum helper. Available in most cities, these unique professionals do light housekeeping (or is it already heavy?) and cooking as well as assist nursing mothers. Ask your childbirth educator for a reference.

You may notice that some people are very free with suggestions even when you haven't asked for any. What's especially irksome is suggestions from people who have no children of their own. Even worse, though, are those that come from Grandma. Those are harder to ignore. If you don't agree with her advice, at least make an effort to ignore it. Remember, you are raising this child—the two of you. The voluntary advisers aren't. You will have to live with the result. So do what you feel is right, what's right for you and your family.

MEETING YOUR OWN NEEDS

After birth, new parents tend to fulfill the needs of the person who screams the loudest first. Usually that's the baby.

Usually, but not always.

New fathers also have needs. Your life is changing. You probably need your partner as much as she needs you.

Most new fathers want to know that they are still loved and still desired, that the baby is not all that matters. No man wants to be second to his child. No father wants to lose his partner's attention. In fact, most extramarital affairs during the postpartum period are the result of lack of attention, not abstention from sex.

You may feel a bit left out. The focus is on the new baby and on the mother. If you've read this far and

*No thanks. I'll be okay if I just rest
for a couple of minutes.*

followed some of the ideas in this book, you may even
feel resentful. Not only are you bringing in a paycheck,
you may be doing a lot of the housework, cooking, and
diaper changing, too. Your sleep is disrupted, your wife
is busy, and you seem to spend a lot of time being
supportive. It's normal to feel resentment if your con-
tributions aren't even noticed, much less appreciated.
Many older people who've raised children don't notice
that fathers weren't always as involved as you are. And
it might feel odd to bring up the subject at work. So
where do you turn?

Talk to your wife. State your position. Let her know how you're feeling. Obviously she will be spending a great deal of time with the new baby, who has almost ceaseless demands. The baby will be the center of attention. But with a little understanding on the part of both parents, they should also be able to meet each other's needs.

Sometimes fathers need support, too. Did you attend a childbirth class? Did you form some friendships there? Were there any men there who felt the same way you did about being a father? Look for a phone number. Many childbirth instructors put out a class roster that lists names and numbers. Maybe your wife has it, or call the instructor. When you get the roster, look it over. Is there anyone on it who looked at things the way you do? Call them. They may be in the same boat and would welcome someone to talk to.

Anyone else? An older brother, an uncle, a good friend? Make it someone who has kids. Remember how much you knew about being a father before you were one. You don't have to have specific questions. Any man who has helped raise children will know where you're coming from.

Finally, look ahead. Your caring enough to spend time with your family now will make a difference. You'll have a happier, healthier child and the satisfaction of knowing that you were on the job when it really counted.

After the first few busy days and weeks have passed, it's important to make time for each other—even if it's just for an hour now and then. Go out for a walk together, to a movie, or to dinner. This can help you both feel less overwhelmed and more in tune with each other.

ADJUSTMENTS

You have planned nine months for this birth and this new human. You've experienced labor, immediately and extremely. Birth and the joy and fulfillment of a new life are past. Two or three days after birth is often a time of inexplicable moods and changing feelings. Not only do you have a new responsibility, but your eating and sleeping habits have been disrupted. It is normal for new dads as well as new moms to have mixed feelings about parenthood. Things will get smoother in time.

After two weeks, the volunteers have left. Grandmas have gone back to their own lives. Now you and your partner have to make both minor and major adjustments.

41

Scheduling can be a real problem. There always used to be time to do the laundry, clean the house, and get the shopping done. But now? When you come home from work, what do you see? An immaculately dusted and vacuumed house, dinner steaming on the stove, and a cooing angelic little bundle from heaven? More likely, you see a vast disorder that resembles a landscape after a tornado and in the center a sleeping and/or nursing madonna and child. Your wife's first hopeful glance is directed at your hands: Do they bear a flat cardboard pizza box? A series of little white containers holding Chinese manna? More likely they are as empty as your hopes for a prepared dinner.

Remember, your wife is not goofing off. She is up often during the night with the baby. If she is nursing, she is spending five to six hours a day holding and feeding. If you're bottlefeeding, she's spending the same amount of time holding, feeding, and preparing. The new person in the house creates an enormous amount of laundry—even if you're using disposable diapers. And finally, she's adjusting to the new situation just as you are. It's difficult.

The new baby sleeps a good deal. When the baby sleeps, it's a good opportunity to do jobs that are impossible to do when the baby is awake. But when the baby awakes, your wife can't take a nap to make up for all the sleep she lost last night, when the baby was also awake. If you are an employer, think about all the necessary adjustments you have to make when you hire someone new. You and your wife just hired someone new. And does he get fringe benefits!

Get together with your wife at a time when you're both awake and the baby's asleep. (Sounds impossible, doesn't it?) Work out some new arrangements. For example, who gets up at night? If she's breastfeeding, you can bring the baby in. Feed him right in bed if that's comfortable for you. It's much more restful for everyone concerned, and neither one of you is going to roll over on the baby in your sleep. Just be sure he's in between you or against a wall. He could roll over the edge. If you're bottlefeeding, Dad can heat and serve as well as Mom. Have you thought about where the baby is at night? Could he sleep beside your bed in a little crib or in a dresser drawer? He'd be instantly retrievable for suckling, and no one would have to get up. Unless, of course, the diaper needs changing—and it always does.

Your wife may be able to nap while she feeds the

I will not admit defeat to
a stupid machine with one chrome dial.

baby during the day. But that usually doesn't make up for the deep sleep most of us enjoy in the dark hours. So she's probably going to be tired. She's probably never before had a job in which she's been on twenty-four-hour call seven days a week and in which her workmate is an incoherent infant. Dad probably has a regular work routine to fall back on and some outside contact. So on the weekends, on your days off, relieve her. Take the baby in your fatherly arms and sing and play with her. She's really pretty neat.

If your partner returns to work after six or eight weeks, it's going to be hard on you both. She won't want to leave the baby, and finding good childcare is often difficult. Unfortunately, however, many households today need two incomes. So her return to work may be unavoidable. Or she may be career-oriented and want to continue her profession.

This can be a troublesome time for both of you. It is not easy to pursue a career and be a parent at the same time. Try to keep your attention zeroed in on the family. Avoid trips, after-hours work, and excessive social engagements. You need time for yourself, time for the two of you who made this marriage, and time for the family. It's an incredible job of juggling emotions, obligations, and responsibilities. Keep your balance. If things begin to seem impossible, talk it out. Your partner and you both need time to talk or just be close. Make sure you do everything in your power to make that happen. Two can juggle better than one.

Whatever the situation, don't forget to make time for one another. Stay close. When you're tired or hassled, it's easy to retreat into a newspaper or book or TV show. And that's necessary—but not all the time. Keep talking. Maybe you can set aside a certain time of the day to be together. If you don't feel chatty, even reading in bed can make you feel closer.

BABY BLUES

Approximately 80 percent of new mothers experience baby blues, a constellation of depression, tears, and irritability, during the first few days or weeks after birth.

Don't be surprised by her tears at inappropriate moments. Don't be surprised by irrationality. Even if you aren't affected, your mate may be.

Baby blues are so common in America that many childbirth professionals believe they are an inevitable part of becoming a parent. Postpartum blues are often attributed to hormonal changes. However, though hormones probably can be implicated, they are not the sole cause of baby blues.

Baby blues are *not* inevitable. A rather startling British study showed that 60 percent of mothers who gave

You think I'm losing my mind, don't you!

birth in hospitals ended up with the blues, while only 16 percent of home-birth mothers reported depression. This doesn't mean that you have to give birth at home to avoid the blues (although many parents find home to be the best place for birth). But it does suggest that the blues do not have to come with every new baby along with the umbilical cord and the placenta.

As already mentioned, the major cause of baby blues is maternal-infant separation. According to Helen Varney, associate professor at Yale University School of Nursing and author of the text *Nurse Midwifery*, "Postpartum blues are largely a psychological phenomenon of the woman who is separated from her family and from her baby."

Another cause is unnatural and peculiar birth customs. The United States is probably the world's leader when it comes to this. The custom of giving birth in a stainless-steel delivery room with machines bleeping and of then whisking the babies away to nurseries immediately after birth is among the most bizarre in the world. No one would ever think of doing that to a goose and her goslings. Why such things are done to people is one of the mysteries of modern obstetrics.

Fortunately, things are changing; obstetrics is shaping up. Unfortunately, innumerable parents still go home from hospitals feeling depressed.

To decrease the likelihood of baby blues, you and your partner should try to remain with the baby during the first hours after birth. Consider early discharge. This is especially important if you are in a hospital that restricts visiting and rooming-in. Separation from the family (as well as from the baby) and/or a prolonged hospital stay (greater than twenty-four hours) often increase the severity of the blues.

There are several other contributing causes of baby blues. Your partner is probably dead tired. She's been a successful homemaker, a competent architect or sales-clerk or teacher. But now she's swamped with new demands. She's not really prepared for that first baby. This is something new and unexpected. It's never been part of her job description. It's not a nine-to-five.

And she's no longer the center of attention. When she was pregnant, the world's attention turned to her. Friends and relatives asked how she was feeling and offered help. Even strangers probably began conversations. Now, suddenly, the focus of attention has shifted to the infant and away from her. It's assumed Mom can cope. It's assumed things are back to normal.

Finally, physical discomforts may contribute to the blues.

You can help by taking a paternity leave, helping out at home, arranging for relatives or friends to assist, and mothering the mother.

Fathers get the blues, too. The house is dirty. Dinner isn't ready, and your mother is coming. Thinking of ways to help will take your mind off the blues. Accomplishment is a remedy for depression. Try it.

Keep busy. Do extra household chores. Talk your feelings out. Find a time when your wife isn't busy(!). Brew a pot of tea. Open a bottle of wine. Talk to other new parents. Remember your childbirth class members. Sometimes talking about your plans for the future will help. Kiss the baby. Feel any better?

Though you can eliminate or relieve the baby blues, don't expect to be able to do away with all the emotional turmoil. That comes along with the placenta and umbilical cord. After the first wave of elation subsides, you may find yourself overwhelmed by the fact that you are a father twenty-four hours a day, seven days a week—forever. You have crossed over the one-way bridge to parenthood. It is not uncommon for a new father to wonder, Am I really cut out to be a dad? Will I be able to supply my family's emotional and spiritual, to say nothing of financial, needs?

Expect to feel a little awkward and unsure at first. It takes time to ease into your new role. It helps to share your feelings with your partner—she's going through it, too.

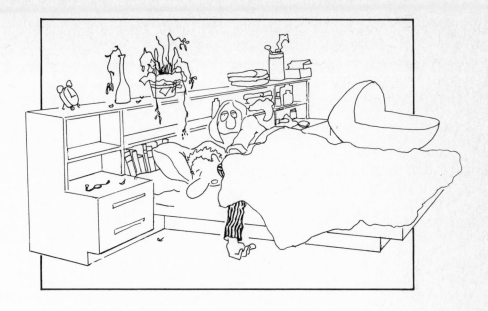

I can't seem to get to sleep, honey.
How about you?

If your partner (or you) is blue, grin and bear it. It's hard, but the best thing about the blues is that they go away. Get through this day and this night. Remember, things get easier every day.

Reassure your wife—and yourself—that your love bond still exists. Don't forget soft words and touches. Be easy on yourself, too. Seek comfort, not new challenges. Try to avoid stressful situations—even though Mr. Stress is living right with you.

If depression persists or seems to be overwhelming one or both of you, seek professional advice. Some childbirth professionals specialize in counseling new moms and dads. Call your childbirth educator for a reference.

GETTING TO KNOW YOU

While you're busy coping with new parenthood, the baby's coping, too. It's rough to be dragged out of a dark, deep sleep into the light and the cold. It's startling to be peered at by oval blobs that continually make cooing noises. And think how a wet diaper—or worse—must feel. It's a wonder babies are as good-tempered as they are.

Your baby recognizes you. She can tell the sound of your voice from others. She may be making little grimaces. Some people say this is gas. But we know better—she's smiling.

Speaking of gas, it's a good idea to know what to do about it. Put a cloth on your shoulder (there are a lot of cloths around by now, aren't there?) and pick up the baby. Keep your hand behind her neck and head for

Daddy hears you. Daddy hears you,
so you must be around here somewhere.

support. Raise her up so she's more or less standing and peering over your shoulder. She'll be kind of sitting on your forearm. Now pat her gently on her back. It's appropriate to bounce her up and down a bit here. Not much though, or you'll find out why you put the cloth on your shoulder. You may find out anyway. You can hear her when she burps. There's nothing polite about a baby.

Playtime for an infant is pretty simple. No point in getting out the electric trains and Barbie dolls; holding your finger out for her to grab is a good game. She'll enjoy it, and so will you. Looking into her eyes and crooning is fun, too. She's the best audience you'll ever have for those vocals you usually do alone in the car. If you're not up to singing, recordings or soothing music can be appropriate. Maybe they'll help you out, too.

She can't see much except for patterns, so elaborate pictures of horsies and doggies aren't needed yet. Something that spins is nice, particularly if it glitters a bit. Just be sure that whatever you leave close enough for her to reach is perfectly safe for an infant.

Have you noticed the little extra tag of tissue left over from her wrapping, the umbilical cord? Looks kind of weird sticking up there, but it'll be gone in a week. You were told it would dry up and go away, and it will. You notice it particularly when you sponge-bathe the baby. It's nice to be in on that. Often newborns are so bundled up, they look more like pillows than people; but under those layers of sweaters and sleepers and blankets, the little person you made is still there.

She doesn't look much like pictures of babies you've seen in magazines and movies. But those aren't real babies—they're actors and models. Your baby probably won't coo and smile all the time and sleep ten hours a night (8 P.M. to 8 A.M.) unless she carries a card from the Screen Actor's Guild. That's not your fault. This is a real baby, and she doesn't follow a script. If other parents tell you tales of their perfect children, take their statements with a grain of salt. Even if they seem to be true, who knows what their children will do with all the malevolence they must be storing up?

As time goes on, you'll probably notice physical changes taking place. The baby's movements grow smoother and less jerky. When she kicks and waves, she no longer resembles Boris Karloff in the first throes of his Frankenstein incarnation. She looks more like a cheerleader in slow motion—definitely more graceful. That froglike fetal posture begins to relax. Her limbs stretch, and when she lies flat, she lies flat. That's a relief. You can quit checking for vestigial gills.

It's hard for new parents to tell when their firstborn is sick. Watch out for high temperatures! Even for short periods they can be dangerous. Call a doctor. Diarrhea and persistent vomiting can be dangerous, too. Diapers are sometimes pretty liquid, but watch out for anything out of the ordinary. A little spitting up is normal, but it should just be a little. Keep an eye on sleeping patterns. If they change drastically, call the baby's caregiver. If anything changes drastically or causes you concern, consult the caregiver. When in doubt, seek professional advice. It's better to be safe than sorry.

Diaper rash, unfortunately, can be an everyday problem. Keep those diapers dry. Your baby's caregiver and your pharmacist can recommend creams and ointments. If you're bottlefeeding, consider switching formula. This can be upsetting for an infant, though; it may cause more problems than it solves. Different brands of disposable diapers have different chemicals in them; try switching brands. Eventually, there will be toilet training—a sure cure.

By the time the baby's a month old, she can raise her head briefly. Put her on her stomach as well as on her back. She can see a lot more in that posture when her head comes up. But watch out—most infants will start to flip over when they're two to three months old. It's easier to do that when you're on your stomach.

Those blue eyes may be changing to brown or black or hazel. Watch for this from three months on. And that lovely hair that she had (maybe) at birth may disappear.

Do you really believe you've become a father?
Just like that?
   Without preparing yourself?
   Without fasting?
   Without gathering moss for
      the birthing bed?
   Without feathers of the wise one
      for your loincloth?

It usually does. Something will replace it, something probably lighter than the eventual hair color. If it's really light, you have one of the classic "bald" babies that Winston Churchill was said to resemble. But that's all right; wasn't he the one who originated the quote about "blood, sweat, and tears"? Your wife and you have certainly lived through that.

It's kind of frightening to think of what's ahead. The little creature perched in your arms will be around for eighteen years or so, and during those years you're going to have to do something you've never done before: Be a parent. We all know how many mistakes parents make—think of your own. You'll probably make mistakes, too, and the worst part of it is that you won't know when you're making them. You're new at this. But so is the baby; she won't notice a lot of them. After all, nobody's perfect.

THE LAYETTE

All the books tell you to shop for a layette, and you don't even know what a layette is? It's a complete outfit of clothing and equipment for the newborn. You and your partner may have bought a lot of baby stuff before the birth. Do you need anything else you don't have? Diapers and baby clothes? Blankets? Crib sheets? Feeding equipment? (If your partner's breastfeeding, she's got this.) Use the list below to check your supplies.

By the way, many parents overdress the baby. It's not necessary to clothe the baby for winter in the arctic when its seventy-three degrees outside. Dress her as you would dress yourself. If you keep your thermostat down and your indoor temperature is cool, dress her with one more layer than the adults in your home wear.

LAYETTE LIST

Furniture and Accessories

- [ ] infant car seat
- [ ] cradle or bassinet
- [ ] 4–6 crib sheets (no need for top sheets)
- [ ] mattress pad
- [ ] infant seat for indoors
- [ ] stroller or carriage
- [ ] cloth baby-carrier
- [ ] secure changing table
- [ ] 4–6 receiving blankets (a small, soft, lightweight blanket used to wrap an infant)
- [ ] 1–2 heavy blankets or a quilt
- [ ] baby bathtub
- [ ] pacifier
- [ ] toys
- [ ] musical mobile

Clothing

- [ ] large box of newborn-size disposable diapers; or
- [ ] 3 dozen cloth diapers with 4–6 diaper pins; or
- [ ] diaper service and diaper pail
- [ ] 4–6 pairs rubber pants
- [ ] 4–6 undershirts
- [ ] 4–6 drawstring gowns (nightgowns that tie at bottom and enclose the baby's feet)
- [ ] 4–6 stretch suits (also called stretchies or jumpsuits; these snap down the front and along the inside of each leg)
- [ ] 1–2 sweaters

Way to go, stud!

- [ ] snowsuit or bunting (a snowsuit has legs; a bunting is a zippered bag with arms, hood, and mittens like a snowsuit, but it has no legs)
- [ ] mittens
- [ ] 1 hat
- [ ] blanket sleeper with feet (zip-up baby sleeping bag, with or without feet)
- [ ] booties or socks
- [ ] bibs

Toilet Articles

- [ ] baby shampoo
- [ ] baby powder
- [ ] baby lotion
- [ ] rubbing alcohol and cotton swabs (to wipe cord stump)

THE GREAT ESCAPE

Been out visiting with baby along? How many trips to the car did it take you? It's hard to believe that someone that small can generate so much extra luggage. There's the diaper bag (usually big enough to serve a full-size person as a two-week suitcase) crammed with diapers, talcum, wiping material, spare pins, and the odd toy or two (God knows why you're carrying around a pint-size football). There's the car seat and the baby carrier. Luckily, the carrier's usually full of baby and attached to someone, so it doesn't have to be carried separately. There are blankets and quilts enough to outfit the Chinese army on a winter expedition. If your mate isn't breastfeeding, that's another bag. How do you move the baby and accoutrements in and out of vehicles? A conveyor belt from the house to the driveway would be one solution. There must be another.

But the trip out is worth it. Everyone loves a new baby. If you're feeling a bit blue and hemmed in, it's nice to get out and be praised for what you've done. People smile at babies, cluck at them, and make cooing sounds under their breath. Strangers walk up and ask about ages. A baby is a sort of passport to good feeling. And do you know why? All those people are remembering when they had babies and what a good feeling it was—at least sometimes. Smile back. Gloat. You get to take the baby home.

Carrying the baby around may be a problem. She's light, but unless you've taken lessons in being one-armed, it's difficult to do anything else but carry. Think about a carrier. (Baby carriers are ancient devices that have been reinvented recently by companies who now make a fortune peddling them to parents who want to do something besides carry babies.) When babies are little, they're usually slung in front in a kind of hammock arrangement—the soft types that cradle her close in front. Find a carrier that's easy to adjust so *you* can carry the little rascal, too. Taking a walk with the baby in the carrier next to your body is one of the best ways a dad can draw close to his baby. And a carrier often works wonders with a crying baby. Many babies will quiet right down once they're in it.

Later, when the baby's neck and back muscles grow stronger, you can use a backpack. This is easier on you than a front carrier, and the baby gets to see over your shoulder. At this stage it's a little hard to visualize a back-carried baby; yours probably has about as much bone structure as a rubber band. But it happens. Check the carrier you select to be sure it is well constructed and safe. The government does not do this for you. If your infant feels heavy after the third tour of the shopping mall or park, think what your wife went through.

Sometimes you're more concerned about people coming in than about you going out. Everyone wants to see the new baby. Don't wear yourself out entertaining, and keep an eye on your partner. She's got a full-time job already and shouldn't have to be a hostess, too. Take it easy, both of you. You can't very well turn away family; if their visits are wearing you out, schedule them. (Check with your wife first.) Your wife can discourage casual dropping in by keeping her nightgown and robe on during the day, if this doesn't make her uncomfortable. If she answers the door dressed this way, most people will take the hint and retire. So she can, too.

Don't forget to go out with your partner, just the two of you. Think about baby-sitting arrangements. The baby's so small that the thought of leaving her with a sitter may be a bit shocking at first. Make the sitter Grandma or Aunt Harriet who have raised children, and make the separation short—maybe an hour or two. If you haven't relatives around, ask parents you know and trust to recommend a sitter. Find someone they trust; it's important.

Make a date. Make it two weeks in advance, call those relatives, and stick to it. Get out together for a movie or a meal. You may feel lost without the new member of the family, but Grandma will love it, and it will do both of you good. Furthermore, make it a regular thing, even if it's only once a month. You made this baby as a couple, and eventually, though it may seem impossible now, you'll be a couple again. Keep your relationship going.

TWIST
AND SHOUT

Do you pick him up every time he cries?" Heard that one yet? It's spoken in just the right tone of voice to imply that your mewling infant is well on his way to a life of spoiled indulgence, a master of welfare cheating. And you did it with your perverse insistence that he be cared for when he's unhappy and very loud about it.

Most experts now say you can't spoil an infant. So lift him up and hold him.

Still crying? Here are some things to do. Check the diaper. Wet, cold pants would make anyone uncomfortable. Is it time to eat? Try the nipple.

So you have a dry, fed, wailing baby. What to do now? It could be gas. How can you tell? Hold the baby upright against your chest so she's looking over your shoulder. Use both hands, one around her bottom and one behind her neck. Pat her gently on the back with the bottom hand. (It's wise to have a cloth or clean diaper over your shoulder—she may spew up a bit.) Listen for a burp. There, that may do it.

No—she's still crying. Try holding her as before and rocking. No rocking chair? Try standing or sitting and pretending you're on a rocking chair. Did that quiet her down?

No, there she goes again. Well, let's walk her up and down a few times, making soothing sounds. "There, there," in a low tone is appropriate here. Or sing her a lullaby. Babies are usually amazed by singing. No rock 'n' roll or opera arias; just a soothing soft song. Whew, she's dropped off!

Lay her down gently in the crib. Damn! The eyes pop open. The face screws up, the fists clench, and there she goes again. Now what?

Repeat all of the above. Or anything. Particularly anything that seemed to work before. Get a book or magazine, find a comfortable chair, and try to read and rock the baby at the same time. If she drops off now, keep trying to put her down. Eventually you'll probably succeed.

If all else fails, you can take her for a ride or for a walk—that is, if you're awake enough. Motion seems to soothe most infants. Whether she's riding in a baby carrier or in a car, she will calm down a bit, and the sandman will call.

If she wakes up when you put her down this time, call your wife.

Some babies are just fussy. Nothing seems to be wrong, but she whines and whimpers—usually right at dinnertime or during that moment you've finally gotten

68

Relax. I'll get your mother to change you.

together again with your spouse. This is hard to take. Walk the baby, and make soothing noises. But if you find yourself getting tense and aggravated, maybe let her fuss for a while.

Some babies are afflicted by colic. Colic can start anytime but usually begins in the first month. The baby fusses a lot; you may think you're doing something wrong. You walk him, you feed him, you rock him, he calms a bit, but then he begins wailing again. Often it only happens during certain times of the day or (worse) at night.

That's right. Getting sleepy . . . sleepy . . . sleepy.

Check for colic. Then do your best to cope. A colicky baby usually pulls his legs up, squints, grimaces, and passes gas. There's not much to do about it. Burp him, soothe him. If he continues, it may be best to put him down for a while. Infants can feel tension. If you pick him up and rock him nervously and restlessly, it won't help him relax. Put him down on his stomach. Take a break. Take a walk. Have a glass of wine. Look at the birds outside. Do your Lamaze breathing. Think of how sweet he really is. When you pick him up again, relax, even though that's difficult when you have a shrieking infant in your arms.

Finally, remember that there are no "bad" babies, only babies who temporarily act like fools. Like gas, this too shall pass.

THE NURSING FATHER

Breast milk arrives in two to four days after the birth. But the baby should be encouraged to nurse right from the start. At first he'll get the thin, watery fluid called colostrum. It's packed with protein and antibodies.

Many infants nurse well the first day; others take a few days to get the hang of it. If the baby is brought to Mom every four hours, as in some hospitals, it is often more difficult to learn. Avoid this. Keep the baby with you. It's yours, not the hospital's. Babies don't have watches. They're hungry when they're hungry, not every four hours.

On the other hand, sometimes infants are awakened from a deep sleep and presented immediately with a swollen nipple. They just don't feel like eating till they're thoroughly awake. If you're rooming-in or are at home, you can have the newborn with you and feed him when he's hungry. That makes it easier for him to learn to nurse. Don't let Mom get discouraged. Breastfeeding is worth working for.

For one thing, the antibodies in colostrum and breast milk make for a healthier baby. The American Academy of Pediatrics recommends breast milk as the primary source of nutrition for the first six months of life. There'll be fewer colds and fewer stomach upsets—and the diapers are bearable. There's no polite word for a formula-fed baby's diaper; breastfeeding infants fill diapers, too, but far less offensively.

Breastfeeding is easy. Your wife has the necessary equipment already. And she can nurse the baby anytime, anywhere. Some parents think it embarrassing to breastfeed. Not today. Breastfeeding moms are becoming a more and more common sight. If you are concerned about discretion, there are many clothes made exclusively for nursing mothers that offer easy access for baby and discretion for Mom. Maternity shops and department stores often offer these, but another good resource for information is La Leche League. Remember, if you think nursing in public is conspicuous, think how much more conspicuous a screaming hungry baby is.

There's a big advantage in breastfeeding for you, too. You might get up at 2 A.M. to carry the baby to bed for feeding, but there's no reason (or way) for you to participate further. And sleep is awfully precious with a little one in the house. If you both need a bit more sleep, bring the hungry insomniac to bed with you.

SUPPORTING
BREASTFEEDING MOM

To make a success of breastfeeding, you must be supportive. There are many ways to help your breastfeeding partner. Encourage her. If breast milk doesn't come in immediately, don't let her frustration stop frequent nursing. The more she nurses, the more quickly it will come in. Remember, she's already producing colostrum, which will give your baby extra proteins and antibodies when he needs them the most.

Encourage your mate to eat well and to drink plenty of fluids. Tell her to rest well. (Never mind the look she gives you.) Tell her how beautiful she looks when she's nursing. Her eyes grow dreamy, and her body relaxes, and her whole presence becomes soft and languid. Before you tell her this, make sure she isn't sleeping.

And nursing doesn't hurt your lovemaking. She's awfully attractive right now, isn't she? Studies about the relationship between breastfeeding and sexual desire suggest that different women have different reactions. But if she isn't too tired (and maybe you can help out there), there's no reason why something, at least, can't get back to normal. You have to stay in practice; you may decide you want another one.

Nursing moms sometimes feel overwhelmed. The new baby demands and gets a lot of skin-to-skin contact, besides being nursed six or so hours a day. By the end of the day, some women are tired of the demands on their bodies. They want to be responsive and sensitive, but deep down they may be saying, "I want my body back! No more demands!" The best way to find out if this is the case is to ask.

In any event, nursing should not interfere with a couple's sexual relationship if each partner is reasonably sensitive to the other's needs.

Some men feel jealous when their partner nurses. "My wife always seemed so attractive, so beautiful, as she sat down to nurse," writes Martin Greenberg. "I felt that I was competing with Jonathan for her attention, and on occasion this was combined with the feeling that I was a little boy. Out of nowhere would come the thought, 'Hey, I want to nurse, too. Move over, Jonathan.' "* Some jealousy is normal. It's not likely to be a problem as long as both new parents are responsive to each other as well as to their baby.

In our culture breasts are an erotic symbol as well as prosaic feeding equipment. One moment you may see your nursing family as an idyllic glowing picture of domesticity and peace; the next day brings twinges of envy. Your wife looks so dreamy and contented; the two of them are so complete in themselves. You may feel left out. That's a normal feeling. Maybe the best thing to do at that moment is to walk over and kiss your wife—and your baby. Be part of the picture.

A generation ago most children were bottlefed in this country, so breastfeeding can seem odd to many males. Just remember, bottles and rubber nipples are a recent invention; generations grew up breastfeeding on this earth before anyone ever heard of formula. And remember, too, if you're saving for that new Porsche, that breast milk is free.

Make the nursing decision together. Bear in mind the many advantages the breastfed baby—and you—

* Martin Greenberg, *The Birth of a Father*. (NY: Continuum, 1985), p. 94.

gain. Although nursing is an exclusively womanly function, there is no reason the man should be isolated. You can nurture your child in other ways. And if you want to feed the baby, your partner can express some milk into a bottle.

If your partner is having any trouble breastfeeding or if either of you just wants information, call your local La Leche League. This organization of experienced nursing mothers offers advice and supports novice breastfeeders at no cost. Check your phone book for your local group. If there is no listing, call the national office for a referral. (See the references at the end of this book.)

BOTTLEFEEDING

If you're bottlefeeding, the most convenient way to hold the baby is in the crook of your arm. There'll be complete instructions on the formula package so you don't have to worry about preparation. When the bottle and its contents are at the correct temperature, apply the nipple to the baby's lips, and he'll do the rest. Elevate the bottle so that the nipple is always full of milk. Otherwise, air is eaten, too, and more burping is involved.

This is hand work. Never prop a bottle on a blanket and leave the baby to eat alone. He's too little to control the bottle, and it could lead to choking or worse. When he's fed, burp him.

LOVEMAKING

Will your love life ever be the same again? Many new fathers wonder about this.

Sexual feelings vary from couple to couple in the weeks and months after the baby is born. Some notice little or no change. Others find their sexual life totally turned around or even nonexistent for a while.

Not everyone waits four to six weeks to resume lovemaking. I know what the doctor said. But unless there are special problems, the best time is when you both feel ready, after the lochia has stopped flowing. Keep checking—or move to France. French doctors suggest waiting only three weeks.

If you do begin lovemaking before the first postpartum exam, it is wise to consult the caregiver to be sure your partner is healing properly.

On the other hand, sometimes it will be months before your love life is back to normal again. You both may be suffering from terminal exhaustion. Your partner may be sore as a result of bruising, tearing, and possibly an episiotomy (a surgical incision to enlarge the birth outlet as the baby is born). However, you will probably be reassured to learn that, far from impairing postpartum recovery, lovemaking actually promotes healing.

You may notice a few changes. The vagina has stretched to pass the baby's head (grapefruit size), but it soon returns to its usual snug shape. To help it along, your partner should do pelvic floor exercises regularly (tightening and contracting the muscles of the pelvic floor as if to stop urination). If she's never tried doing this particular exercise during lovemaking, she should. You both might be amazed. Sometimes muscles are wonderful things.

Some mothers are nervous about intercourse the first time after giving birth. Go easy. She may be quite sore at first.

Sexual reactions may be a bit slowed. It may take your parner longer to become sexually stimulated as a result of hormonal changes. This is temporary. It may also take her longer to achieve orgasm. Or she might find orgasm less satisfying. You can both try to enjoy nonorgasmic intercourse for a while. And remember, lovemaking doesn't always have to include intercourse. There are other roads to sexual fulfillment: caressing, fondling, manual stimulation of the breasts and clitoris, oral stimulation of the breasts, and fellatio.

Temporary changes in lovemaking patterns are quite common. They don't mean anything is wrong. Rest assured—things will no doubt get back to normal again.

One additional thing must be mentioned. Babies are fond of waking and wailing at inopportune moments. This is one of them. Maybe he can go to sleep in another room—or maybe on the other side of town. You can try surrounding yourself with a screen of music, but music louder than a baby's crying is sometimes not conducive to romance, either. Be patient, and thank God there'll be other times.

Finally, be aware that new mothers are not impregnable. Nursing moms can conceive. To postpone siblings, some couples use lubricated condoms, diaphragm jelly, or foam because those methods provide added moisture and promote comfort and pleasure as well as contraception. (Diaphragms and cervical caps are best fitted after recovery is complete.) Talk it over with your wife.

It's just as important to keep the physical current going as the emotional—maybe more so right now. You're both under a lot of stress. You need a little comfort.

THE ROCK OF GIBRALTAR

Will I be a good dad?" How
many fathers have asked themselves that question? It's
an awesome responsibility, being in charge of someone
else's life. For the next eighteen years (and maybe
longer), you and your wife will complete the charge you
have assumed—to raise a healthy human, a new link in
the chain of life on our earth. Anyone would feel nervous faced with such a task; no one is ever going to do
a perfect job.

How do you strike the balance between discipline
and love? If we had been unfettered and left to our own
devices while growing up, most of us would have become utterly obnoxious. How can you instill compas-
sion and common sense into a growing child? By

Hey, Bozney! Will you get with it—
he's gaining on us again!

practicing them yourself. Most emotional learning is imitation. If you show in your actions the qualities you think important, your child will follow your lead. Not always and not exactly, but close enough.

Studies have shown that children who grew up in a situation where both Mom and Dad provided love and care do better in school and are likely to become involved parents themselves when their time comes. Those studies aren't surprising: all living things respond to attention. And we often tend to imitate our parents— at least, when we finish reacting against them. If you've admired the way some man you know behaves as a father (a friend, your own father), take a good look at what he does or did. What kinds of attention work? Will they work for you? Are you comfortable offering them? Nobody can change their personality type and expect it to be genuine, but if you see something you like, you can generally make it work. Ask for advice. But remember that the things that work for one person sometimes don't work for another. When in doubt, let yourself be guided by love. That's what guided you into childbirth in the first place.

Then there's the question of physical discipline. With an infant, of course, it doesn't arise. But as children grow older, they've got to be protected from themselves: an eight-month-old must be kept away from electrical outlets. If you wish to raise someone who will use reason and not violence, you must refrain from violence yourself. Stern words to an older child or a firm no to a younger will usually do the trick. We've come a long way from days when parents routinely beat their children into obedience.

If you wish to raise someone who is emotionally secure, you must give them emotional security from the beginning. When you punish him for bad behavior, always make sure the child knows it's the behavior that's being punished, not the person. Children are rational creatures part of the time; they can usually see your point. Everyone needs people they can trust. See that the trust an infant has in Mom and Dad is earned and justified as that infant grows.

87

No way . . . couldn't be a heart attack . . .
he wouldn't be snoring.

Maybe you have money worries or think you might in the future. An infant is relatively inexpensive (after you've covered the medical expenses), but the bigger a person gets, the more they consume. Unless you're independently wealthy, you'll probably have these thoughts now and then. Try to keep them to a minimum. The best investment you can make for your child's security and future is the love and care and attention you give now. Money has surprisingly little to do with developing a healthy human. It would be wise to keep your work hours short and your home hours long. Avoid extra commitments. It's more important to return from work in a good frame of mind and relieve Mom than it is to bring in extra bucks. Now that you're a father, you may be tempted to take on community service jobs or get more involved in your church. Resist this if you can. Get rid of extra obligations if at all possible. Don't start going to law school at night now. Wait a year. Right now, you and your energies are needed at home. There will be time later, when the baby's older and routine returns to family life. It may seem as if routine will never return, but it will. Honest.

THE CESAREAN FATHER

C-section. That's the term you're likely to hear in the hospital from nurses and doctors. A C-section is a surgical incision into the uterus so that the baby may be born. Often cesareans are performed while labor is in progress, sometimes after many hours of labor. If the labor has been difficult, a cesarean may seem a blessing. So it is, in a way. It allows the relatively safe birth of an infant who might otherwise be in trouble. But it creates problems, too.

The cesarean mother is in a unique situation. She must recover both from major abdominal surgery and from birth. She must take care of another while she is still in need of care herself. If your wife has had a C-section, she will need even greater support from you.

Dads as well as moms have strong reactions to cesarean births. At first, many fathers feel relieved that labor is over and the baby is healthy. The same joyful emotions that crown vaginal birth often follow a cesarean delivery: pride, elation, and fulfillment. But almost invariably, negative feelings intrude. It's not uncommon for Dad to feel deprived and sorrowful: birth didn't happen the way it should. It's not uncommon for new cesarean moms to feel that their bodies have let them down, that they've somehow done something wrong. Grief is an appropriate reaction to cesarean surgery.

Both parents often suffer from *surgical birth trauma.* This includes the new mother's physical discomfort, interruption of the normal parent-infant attachment process, emotional suffering, breastfeeding difficulties, and an increased financial burden. What can you do to smooth this rocky road?

Make sure you're there for the birth. You don't have to witness the operation. You'll be seated near your partner's head, and a screen will block out the actual surgery. Of course, if you want to see the birth, you can simply stand up. Hold her hand, smooth her brow, and reassure her. Your presence will help you both focus on the birth, not on the operative procedure. It will reduce your partner's anxiety and promote attachment with your child afterward.

Most cesareans are unplanned and unexpected. The decision to perform surgery is made during labor. Because of this, every couple should choose a hospital that encourages father participation during the operation— just in case.

Two types of anaesthesia are used for cesareans. Regional anaesthesia means that Mom can be awake during the surgery. General anaesthesia means she will be unconscious. Many mothers choose regional so that they will be awake for the birth and because it's relatively safer. In many hospitals fathers aren't permitted in the delivery room if general anaesthesia is used, but even if this is the case, try to be there anyway. You can later share the birth with your wife.

Hold your baby close to Mom immediately after birth. That way your wife can see the baby, establish eye contact, touch him with her face and fingertips, and smell the fresh odor of the newborn. No physician will perform surgery in a dimly lit room (we hope). However, cupping your hand just above the infant's sensitive eyes may encourage him to open them.

If there is an emergency that requires immediate pediatric care, make up for lost time with the baby as soon as you are both able.

IN THE RECOVERY ROOM

When surgery is complete (after about an hour), your partner will be taken to a recovery room, where she will remain for two to three hours until the anaesthesia wears off and her condition is stabilized.

If the mother has had general anaesthesia, she may be quite groggy for a while. Needless to say, she will not be able to enjoy contact with the baby until after the anaesthesia wears off. However, if she has had regional anaesthesia, she can experience immediate contact with the baby.

Remain together with the baby to continue the ongoing process of parent-infant attachment. Bear in mind that the parent-infant relationship has been severely traumatized by the fact of surgery. Use every opportunity you can to make the follow-up as normal as possible under the circumstances.

THE POST-CESAREAN HOSPITAL STAY

The average hospital stay after a cesarean is three to seven days.

In some hospitals the father can remain twenty-four hours after a cesarean, as well as after a vaginal birth. This, of course, is the ideal. Unfortunately, however, it is not very common. Whether you stay with your partner twenty-four hours a day or come and go, you will find the following beneficial:

■ Take the lion's share of baby care. Hold, nurture, diaper, and bathe the baby. Of course, there are nurses available to do this. But it is important for *you* to care for your baby. This will make your own transition to fatherhood smoother. In addition, it will lessen some of the trauma of cesarean birth for the family.

■ Help your partner feel comfortable. Adjust the bed, adjust the pillows, give her a back massage, or brush her hair if she wishes.

■ Help her walk around. This promotes healing. A nurse should be present the first time the mother is up.

■ Help your partner with nursing. Breastfeeding is just as important for the cesarean-born baby as it is for the vaginally born child. In fact, it is probably even more important. But for the cesarean mother it may be uncomfortable.

You can help by bringing the baby to the mother and helping her adopt a nursing position of comfort. Two comfortable positions for cesarean mothers are:

Side-lying, with the baby cradled in the mother's arms facing her, pillows supporting her back, belly, and perhaps upper leg. When your mate has finished nursing from one breast, you can take the baby and let her roll over so she can nurse from the other.

Sitting up with bended knees to lessen the strain on the abdomen and a pillow over the stitches.

HOMECOMING

Since the hospital stay for a cesarean birth is longer than for a normal birth, there will be a more difficult adjustment at home. To make the transition smoother:

■ Arrange for help. The help of relatives and/or friends can mean a great deal to cesarean parents.

■ Discuss your feelings together. Confronting feelings is necessary for complete healing. Many fathers feel that they have failed their partners. Perhaps they think they did not give adequate labor support or failed to "protect" them sufficiently from medical intervention. Mothers also often feel that they have failed their mates. Working through these feelings takes time. But time will heal.

■ Don't hesitate to contact a support group like Cesareans/Support, Education and Concern, which offers help to cesarean families. (See the listings on page 134 for information.)

Many childbirth professionals fail to understand the emotional aspects of surgical birth trauma. They naïvely assume that it doesn't matter how the baby is born, as long as he is healthy. But for most parents the mode of delivery *is* important.

Meanwhile, relatives and friends often make thoughtless remarks to the new cesarean mother, such as "you took it the easy way." How anyone can imagine that major abdominal surgery is easier than a natural birth is a mystery.

Above all, remember that though a great gulf separates a cesarean from a normal birth, there is also a world of difference between a cesarean and any other operation.

A child is born.

FOOD FOR THOUGHT: RECIPES

©BLAINE 1984

If you haven't been doing much cooking, it may take a little practice to get used to it again. Here are some suggested menus for the first ten days.

DAY ONE RECIPE

Steak

1   tablespoon each butter and oil
1   pound steak (New York, porterhouse, or T-bone)
    salt
    pepper
½ pound mushrooms, sliced
½ cup red wine
    baked potatoes, and/or French bread (sliced, buttered, reassembled, wrapped in aluminum foil, and baked in a 350° oven for 20 minutes)

You deserve this. If you enjoy wine, buy a good red and use it in the recipe—it'll make a difference. Put the butter and oil in a frying pan, heat to a sizzle. Cook the mushrooms 5 minutes. Remove. Add the steaks (dry them first, then add salt and pepper). Sear quickly on both sides to a nice gold color, then turn the heat to moderate (halfway between high and simmer), and cook for 5–10 minutes more, to your taste. You can cut into one to check redness inside. When the steaks are done, remove them and slosh a little bit of wine into the pan. Cook over high heat till the juices are syrupy, and pour the mushrooms and juice over the steak. Serve with potatoes or French bread and a salad of lettuce, green pepper, and tomato.

Sweet and Sour Tofu

1 cake tofu, cut in 1-inch squares
2 tablespoons oil
1–2 cloves garlic, minced
3 slices ginger root, minced
2 carrots, cut in thin diagonal slices
1 onion, cut in chunks
1 green pepper, sliced thin

Sauce:

½ cup chicken broth
½ cup white vinegar
1 tablespoon tomato paste (or ketchup)
1 tablespoon soy sauce
3–4 tablespoons brown sugar
1½ tablespoons cornstarch mixed with three
  tablespoons chicken broth

Combine all the sauce ingredients except the corn-starch mixture. Heat in a saucepan until bubbling. Add the cornstarch mixture, stirring constantly until the sauce is thick. Keep warm until served.

 Cook the tofu in boiling water until the squares rise to the top. Strain them, and set them aside.

 Sauté the garlic and ginger in the oil in large frying pan over medium heat for 1 minute. Add the carrots, onion, and pepper. Stir-fry for 2-3 minutes. Add the tofu and sauce. Mix gently, and serve with rice.

Italian Pork Chops

2   pork chops, ¾ inches thick
2   tablespoons oil (olive oil, if possible)
2   bay leaves
1   teaspoon rosemary
    pepper
    salt
¼   cup white wine (or water, but wine is better)
    rice *or* Italian bread

Dry the pork chops with a paper towel. Brown them
in the oil over high heat with the bay leaves, rosemary, salt, and a dash of pepper. When they brown
on one side, turn them; then add more rosemary and
pepper. Keep cooking till they're very brown. Then
add the white wine and cover. Lower the heat to
simmer, and tip the pan around to spread the juices.
Simmer till the steaming noise stops (5-10 minutes).
Uncover and let some wine evaporate (5 more minutes). Serve with Italian bread or rice. Pour the pan
juices over everything—they're good. Serve with
frozen green beans or a green salad.

Tuna Casserole

2   quarts water
6½- ounce can tuna
      can of cream of mushroom or cream of
      chicken soup
8   ounces egg noodles

Put water on to boil in a big pot. Open the tuna and the soup and mix them in a bowl big enough to hold four cups of noodles. When the water boils, add the egg noodles. When it reboils, turn the heat down so the water won't foam over the top. Simmer (bubbling steadily) for 8 minutes. Drain the noodles in a collander. In a casserole dish add the tuna/soup mixture to the noodles. Mix together. Eat it now, or put in a 350° oven for a half hour. Add cheese to the top, if you like. This can be rewarmed in the oven. Serve with frozen or canned peas on the side, or add them to the casserole.

Hamburgers

½–1 pound ground beef
1   tablespoon oil
      frozen French fries, if you like

Shape the ground beef into two patties. Fry them
over high to medium heat in a little bit of oil for about
5-10 minutes to a side. Or you can broil them three
inches from the heat, 10 minutes on one side, turn,
then 5 minutes on the other. Oven French fries are
easy with this; they usually go on a baking pan 20
minutes at 400°.

   To make these fancier, make four thin patties. On
two of them, put a slice of cheese or a slice of fried
bacon or sliced fried pepperoni or sliced avocado and
cooked ham. Cover with the other patties, seal the
edges by pinching them together, and cook as above.
Serve with potato chips or French fries, tomato, and
lettuce.

Oven-Baked Fish

3 tablespoons margarine
¾ pound fish filets (cod or other firm, white-
  fleshed fish)
  lemon juice, white wine, or sherry
  salt
  pepper

Preheat the oven to 425°. Put a shallow pan in to
preheat. Remove the pan, and add the margarine.
Swirl to melt. Add the fish, and turn them to coat
them with the margarine. Return to the oven and
bake uncovered until the fish flakes easily (about 10
minutes if fish is 1 inch thick). You can sprinkle a
little lemon juice, white wine, or sherry onto the fish
first if you like. Add salt and pepper when it is done.
Serve with rice and green beans.

Macaroni and Cheese

3   tablespoons margarine
3   tablespoons flour
1½ cups milk
½   teaspoon dry mustard
1   teaspoon salt
     pepper
     hot sauce
8   ounces macaroni
3   quarts water
2   cups grated cheddar cheese
     cut-up hot dogs or sausage or ham

Melt the margarine in a saucepan. Add the flour, and
stir together. (This will look like kind of a loose
dough; it's called a roux.) Cook for 3 minutes over
moderate heat. Add the milk, and stir well so there
are no lumps. If there are, too bad. Add the mustard,
the salt and pepper, and a dash of hot sauce. Heat to
bubbling over high heat, stirring constantly. Turn the
heat off. Simmer the macaroni in the boiling water for
10 minutes, then drain. (Don't add the macaroni till
the water is boiling; time it from when the water
returns to a boil.) While this cooks, grate your cheese
and add it to the milk sauce. Mix the drained macaroni and the sauce together in a big casserole or dish,
and bake at 350° for half an hour. Add the cut-up
meat before you bake, if you like. (You can just buy
cheddar cheese soup and add this to macaroni after
it's cooked.) Serve with a green salad.

Meatloaf

2 slices bread
¼ cup milk
1 pound ground beef
¼ pound sausage (sometimes called country or
    breakfast sausage)
1 egg
4 tablespoons minced onion (the dried kind
    from a jar will work fine)
    dash of Worcestershire sauce
    spices: a sprinkle of rosemary, oregano,
    thyme, garlic, sage, and two medium-sized
    potatoes

Soak the bread in the milk for a few minutes. Then
pull it apart into little pieces. Mix this and everything
else except the potatoes together and form into a loaf.
You may want to take your rings off before you do
this. Put the loaf into a bread pan or a baking dish
with high sides to keep the grease from spilling out,
and bake for an hour at 350°. Put the potatoes in at
the same time. Wash them and prick them with a
fork; they won't explode in the oven that way. Pour
the grease off the meatloaf after an hour (use a spent
soup can; don't pour it down the sink), and return it
to the oven. Cook the meatloaf and potatoes for another half hour. Serve with fresh, canned, or frozen
corn (follow package directions) and a lettuce and
tomato salad.

Ham

1, 3, or 5	pounds canned ham
2	tablespoons dry mustard
½	cup brown sugar
1	can sliced pineapple

Canned hams often come with cooking instructions. Follow them, or bake it fat side up at 350° for 1½ hours in a baking pan. Use a rack to keep the ham out of its drippings. The last half hour, you can glaze the ham, if you like. Remove the ham from the oven, and score it by making shallow cuts across it at right angles, one inch apart. Mix the dry mustard and the brown sugar with the drippings or with the juice of the can of pineapple. Spoon this mixture onto the ham. You can lay some of the pineapple slices on the ham, too, for the last half hour. A 5-pound ham will feed you four or five times. Slice it cold, reheat it, fry it. Freeze it in a plastic sack; it'll last a month or two at 0°. Serve with baked potatoes or sweet potatoes and peas.

Filipino Chuck Roast

2 onions, cut in chunks
6 cloves garlic
4 tablespoons lime or lemon juice
⅓ cup soy sauce
3 tablespoons Worcestershire sauce
3 pounds chuck roast
½ cup flour
¼ cup oil
4 potatoes, peeled and quartered
½ cup water

Put the onions, garlic, lime or lemon juice, soy sauce, and Worcestershire sauce into a blender. Puree. Pour over the chuck roast, cover, and leave it in the refrigerator overnight (or at least 3 hours). Take the meat out, dry it with paper towels, flour it, brown it in a heavy pot (a Dutch oven is ideal), and take it out. Put two tablespoons of the oil in the pot; brown potatoes; take them out. Return the meat and the marinade, add water, boil, cover, and simmer one hour. Add the potatoes, and simmer one more hour. Serve with fresh, canned, or frozen corn and a green salad.

No, Edith. Telling him fabric softener is on aisle
thirteen was bad enough, but going around the
other way to watch his futile search is really sick.

SNACKS

Stock up on yogurt and cottage cheese. Get some good
slicing cheese and plenty of fresh fruit. How about
roasting a turkey and slicing up the leftovers? You can
slice raw vegetables (carrots, celery, broccoli, cauli-
flower) and keep them in a plastic container in the refrigerator. These are all good, quick, nutritious snacks.

If you wish to continue cooking, or if none of the recipes for the first ten days appeals to you, here are some further suggestions. They are arranged according to the main ingredient.

Fried Marinated Chicken

¼ cup rum
¼ cup soy sauce
¼ cup lime juice (fresh squeezed is best, but bottled is okay)
3 pounds chicken or chicken pieces
½ cup flour
¼ cup oil

Mix the rum, soy sauce, and lime juice together. Add the chicken pieces. If you bought a whole chicken, you'll have to take it apart. Turn the pieces to coat them with the mixture, then let it sit for 2 hours. Dry it with paper towels. Put the flour on a plate, add chicken pieces, turn to coat, and shake off the extra. Fry floured pieces in oil in frying pan to a deep brown (about 8 minutes). Turn the pieces; fry on the other side. This goes well with rice.

Baked Chicken

1½ pounds chicken breasts, thighs, or
    drumsticks
    salad oil
    rice or frozen French fries

Skin (if you like) and dry the chicken pieces. Oil
lightly a cookie sheet or shallow baking pan, and put
the chicken on it. Bake a half hour at 400°, turn with
tongs, and cook another half hour. Serve with rice or
French fries.

Barbecued Marinated Chicken

3   garlic cloves, peeled
1   cup oil
2   hot chili peppers
1   teaspoon salt
¼   cup lemon juice
3   pounds chicken pieces

Put the garlic and half the oil in a blender. Cut the
stems off the peppers, slit them down the side, and
remove the seeds. Do this under running water, and
don't touch your eyes until you've washed your
hands thoroughly. Add peppers to blender, whirl to a
runny paste. Put this in a rectangular baking dish.
Add the other half of the oil, the salt, and the lemon
juice. Mix. Add the chicken pieces, turn to coat,
marinate 2 hours. Barbecue 15–20 minutes, basting
with the marinade.

Chicken and Sausages

1 onion, sliced
¼ cup oil
3 pounds chicken pieces
  salt
  pepper
½ cup flour
8- ounce package frozen pork sausages
2 cups beer

Fry the sliced onion in the oil till it's limp. Remove
from pan. Dry the chicken pieces, salt and pepper
them, and coat them with flour. Put chicken in pan,
fry to brown, turn, and brown the other side. Put the
chicken and onion in a casserole (a large covered pot
that can go in the oven). Cook the sausages following
the package directions, and add them to the casserole.
Put the beer in the frying pan and scrape the brown
bits in. You may have to heat the frying pan to get
most of them. Pour this mixture in the casserole.
Cover, bake at 350° for 50 minutes, uncover, and turn
oven to 425° for 10 minutes. Serve with rice.

Quick Quiche

2 eggs
1 cup cream
  salt
  pepper
¼ cup shredded Swiss cheese
1 frozen pie shell, nine inches across

Beat together the eggs, cream, and a little salt and
pepper; then add the cheese. Pour this into the pie
shell. Bake at 350° for 35-40 minutes. To see if it's

done, put a knife blade in the center. If it comes out clean, it's done. (You can fry up a couple of slices of bacon crisp and crumble them into the bottom of the pie crust before you add the egg mix, or a can of crabmeat or tuna. Try frying 2 big sliced onions slowly in butter for 15 minutes till they turn sweet, and use this as a base.)

Chicken Tortilla Casserole

3   chicken breasts
1   cup water
1   can cream of mushroom soup
2   seven-ounce cans green chili sauce
1   cup milk
1   dozen corn tortillas
    butter or margarine
1   can sliced ripe olives
¾ pound shredded cheddar cheese
2   tablespoons chopped onion

Cook the chicken breasts in the water. Cool. Take the meat off the bones and cut it into bite-size bits. Mix the same water with the soup and sauce and the milk. Cut the tortillas into 2-inch-square pieces. Put half of these in a buttered 13" x 9" x 2" baking dish. (Take a cube of butter or margarine and rub it quickly around the sides and bottom of the dish.) Add half the chicken pieces and half the olives. Repeat with remaining tortilla bits, chicken, and olives. Pour the soup mixture over all. Top with the cheese and the onion. Bake for one hour at 350°. (This is pretty impressive and will easily feed four people. You can refrigerate it overnight if you make it the day before. Serve with canned refried beans and a salad.)

Tacos

½ pound ground beef
8- ounce can tomato sauce
½ teaspoon oregano
¼ teaspoon cumin
  dash of hot sauce
  tortillas
1 cup grated cheddar cheese
  a few lettuce leaves, sliced
1 small tomato, diced

Fry the beef till it's brown, crumbling it up with a
spatula. Pour off the grease (but not down the drain).
Add the tomato sauce, oregano, cumin, and hot
sauce. Heat the tortillas over a gas flame using tongs.
Fill them with meat mix, then top with cheese, lettuce, and tomato. You can also add sour cream,
chopped olives, chilis, sliced avocado, etc. If you
don't have a gas stove, heat the tortillas by wrapping
them in foil, first sprinkling with a few drops of water, and heating them in a 350° oven for a half hour.

Hash and Eggs

1   can corned beef hash
2–4 eggs

Open the hash at both ends of the can and push it
out into a frying pan. Chop it up with a spatula and
cook on high heat till it smells good (6 minutes or so).
Turn it over. Make some pockets in it with your
spatula, and carefully break the eggs into them. Cover
the frying pan, and turn the heat down to simmer.
Cook about 8 minutes, till the eggs are done the way
you like them.

Baked Beans

2 cups dried beans (pinto or red)
1¼ quarts water
¼ pound salt pork (or bacon), sliced
¼ cup brown sugar
1 teaspoon salt
1 teaspoon dry mustard
3 tablespoons molasses

Wash the beans; bring them to boil in the water for 2 minutes. Remove them from heat, cover, and leave for at least one hour. Add the sliced pork, boil, reduce the heat to simmer, and cook 1 hour covered. Pour off the liquid; save 2 cups of it. To that 2 cups, add the brown sugar, salt, mustard, and molasses. In a casserole, layer the beans and pork. Pour the sugar mix over it, cover, bake 6 hours at 300°. If it dries out (check every 2 hours), add water. This is a lot of trouble, but it makes lots, it's cheap, and it freezes.

Stir-Fried Asparagus (or Broccoli) and Tofu

1 cake tofu, cut in 1-inch squares
2 slices ginger root, minced
1 clove garlic, minced
2 tablespoons oil
1 pound broccoli or asparagus, cut in one- or two-inch lengths
¼ cup water
1 tablespoon soy sauce
1 tablespoon oyster sauce (or sherry)
½ teaspoon sugar
1 teaspoon sesame oil (optional)

Cook the tofu in boiling water until the squares rise to the top, drain, and set aside. In a large frying pan, sauté the ginger and garlic in the oil for 1 minute over high heat. Add the asparagus (or broccoli), and stir-fry 1 minute. Add the water, soy sauce, oyster sauce, sugar, and tofu. Simmer, covered, for 5 minutes (vegetables should be crisp). Add optional sesame oil. Serve with rice. If you want a thicker sauce, stir in ½ teaspoon cornstarch mixed with 1 tablespoon water; simmer, stirring gently, until sauce is thick.

Pasta with Sauce

Cook a package of spaghetti, following the package directions. For optimal nutrition, use whole wheat or vegetable-based spaghetti.

Use any of the following four sauces:

Pesto:

2 cups fresh basil leaves
2 cloves garlic
2 tablespoons Parmesan cheese
3 ounces pine nuts (optional; I often use walnuts)
¾ cups olive oil

Grind the first four ingredients in blender or Cuisinart. Add the oil till the sauce reaches the proper consistency. It should be no thinner than peanut butter. Add more garlic if you like.

Clam sauce:

1   clove garlic
3   tablespoons olive oil
¼   cup white wine
1   six-ounce can minced clams, drained
    salt
    pepper
1   tablespoon chopped parsley

Cook the garlic in the oil till golden; discard the clove. Add the wine and clams and cook over medium-high heat till the wine evaporates (3–5 minutes). When the aroma doesn't tickle your nose anymore, the wine is evaporated. Add salt and pepper to taste; add parsley and simmer five minutes.

Alla Marinara (sailor style):

1   clove garlic
1   red pepper pod, seeded
¼   cup olive oil
3   cups plum tomatoes
½   teaspoon oregano
    salt
1   tablespoon chopped parsley
6   tablespoons Parmesan cheese

Cook the garlic and the red pepper in the oil till the garlic is golden and the pepper is deep brown. Discard them. Cool the pan slightly, and add the tomatoes, crushing them. Add the oregano, boil, then simmer for 20 minutes. Add salt and the parsley. Add the cheese after you've sauced the pasta.

All'ortica (nettle style):

⅓ cup olive oil
¾ pound mushrooms, thinly sliced
3   tablespoons chopped parsley
3   tablespoons lemon juice
    salt
    pepper

Cover the bottom of a frying pan with *some* of the oil.
Sauté the mushrooms 3 minutes. Add half the parsley
and cook 2 minutes; remove from heat. Add the
lemon juice. In a separate pan, heat the remaining oil.
Put the cooked pasta on a serving dish, add the
mushroom sauce, the rest of the parsley, the heated
olive oil, and salt and pepper; mix well and serve.

Cheese Chile Rellenos

1   seven-ounce can whole green chilis
2   cups grated jack cheese
2   eggs
1   cup milk
    salt
    pepper
1   seven-ounce can green chili sauce

Slit the chilis down one side. Stuff as much cheese
into each one as will fit. Lay the chilis in a greased
pan, seams down. Beat the eggs and milk together
with a little salt and pepper. Pour this mixture on the
stuffed chilis and top with any remaining cheese.
Bake at 375° for 40 minutes. Ten minutes before
they're ready, heat the green chili sauce in a saucepan. Pour this on top when you serve.

Shrimp Salad with Avocado

1 celery stalk
¾ pound shrimp meat (pink, already cooked;
    don't use canned shrimp)
½ teaspoon salt
    pepper
1 tablespoon lemon juice
½ cup mayonnaise
1 onion, minced (optional)
1 avocado, ripe and soft
    a little lettuce

Cut the celery into ¼-inch dice; mix with the shrimp.
Add the salt, pepper, and lemon juice, then the mayonnaise. Mix gently so the shrimp don't break. Add
the optional onion here—just a little, to taste. Slice an
avocado lengthwise into halves, open, and discard the
seed. Scoop your shrimp mixture into the seed cavity
and add some lettuce.

Chicken Salad

3 chicken breasts
1 or 2 stalks celery
½ cup mayonnaise
½ cup sour cream
    salt
    pepper

Follow directions for Chicken Tortilla Casserole to fix
the chicken squares. (Save the broth, and use it to
cook rice or noodles in.) Cut the celery into small
pieces. Mix the mayonnaise and sour cream (or use all
mayonnaise or all sour cream); add the chicken, celery, and salt and pepper to taste. You can also add
chopped almonds or peanuts, sliced stuffed olives,

chopped dill pickle, bean sprouts, or little pieces of green pepper. For taste changes, add a little of one ofthe following: curry powder, dill, oregano, sage, or ginger.

Puerco Carlos

This is a spicy, *hot*, and very delicious dish.

Ingredients to be blended together:

1	tablespoon whole cumin seeds
½	tablespoon whole coriander seeds
1	large or 2 small tomatoes
1–2	green chilis
1–2	cloves garlic (optional)
1	large or 2 small onions
½	cup vinegar
4	pork chops, cut thick
1	tablespoon capers

Roast the cumin over high heat in a frying pan. Keep shaking the seeds till they begin to turn dark and smell good. Do the same with the coriander. But be careful—coriander burns easily. Dry grind the roasted spices in a blender then add the other ingredients to be blended together. Add the chopped tomatoes first. Add just enough vinegar to work the blender. (You may not have to add any if the tomatoes are juicy.) Blend to a smooth paste. Brown the chops in enough oil to film the bottom of a deep frying pan. Set them aside. Fry the paste in the same oil (if not burned) over high heat for 5-10 minutes without letting it stick to the pan. Add the pork chops and the remaining vinegar. Sprinkle capers on top. Cover and cook over low heat for 1 hour.

Glazed Pork

2 pounds pork, cut in cubes
¼ cup oil
1 cup minced onion
1 cup orange juice (frozen is okay)
¼ cup lime juice
¼ cup water
¼ teaspoon thyme
½ teaspoon salt
½ teaspoon pepper

Brown the pork in the oil; add the onion, orange juice, lime juice, water, and spices. Cover and bring to a boil. Lower the heat to simmer for 30 minutes. Uncover, boil for 10 minutes, constantly stirring, till the sauce glazes (gets thick and shiny). Serve with rice.

Pork Chili Rojo

2 pounds pork, cubed
¼ cup oil
2 cups water
4 tablespoons chili powder
1 teaspoon salt
2 cloves garlic, minced
4 medium potatoes, peeled and diced

Brown the pork in the oil; pour off most of the fat. Add the water, the chili powder, the salt, and the garlic; cover and boil. Then lower the heat and simmer for 35 minutes. Add the potatoes; cover, boil, and lower the heat to simmer. Simmer 25 minutes.

Italian Chuck Roast

3   slices bacon
1   stalk celery
1   onion
1   carrot
2   tablespoons olive oil
3–4 pounds chuck roast
1½   teaspoons salt
1   cup red wine
1   tablespoon flour
1   cup water

Mince the bacon, celery, onion, and carrot. Heat the olive oil in a Dutch oven or heavy casserole dish, and add the minced mixture. Cook 5 minutes, till brown. Add the chuck roast; cook, turning, 10 minutes or so till brown. Add salt and wine; cook 5 minutes. Add flour mixed with water, stir, and cover tightly. (It helps to put a piece of brown paper [old shopping bag is fine] between the lid and the pot.) Bring to a boil, then turn down to lowest point. Cook at least 2 hours. Check now and then to see if you need to add water. Meat will be spoon-tender. Sauce can be used on spaghetti or Italian bread.

. . . so your wife's check cashing card couldn't
possibly *cover you, too. And for your safety and
convenience you just fill out this simple application
and mail it to our district headquarters.*

Swedish Chuck Roast

1 tablespoon butter
2 tablespoons salad oil
4 pounds chuck roast
1 cup minced onion
3 tablespoons flour
1 tablespoon corn syrup (or brown sugar)
2 tablespoons white vinegar
2 cups beef stock (use beef bouillon cubes)
1 bay leaf
6 anchovies
1 teaspoon peppercorns

Heat the butter and oil in a heavy casserole dish; add
the roast, brown it, and remove it from the pot. Add
the onions and brown. Off heat, add the flour and
stir. Add corn syrup or brown sugar, vinegar, stock,
bay leaf, and anchovies. (Rinse them first.) Add the
meat. Put the peppercorns in a square of cheesecloth,
and tie the top so they can't escape, then crush them
with a knife blade. Add them to the casserole. Cover,
bring to boil on stovetop, then put in a 350° oven for
2½ hours. Remove cheesecloth bag, bay leaf, and
meat; taste the sauce for seasoning. If the sauce is
very thin, boil on stovetop to desired thickness. Serve
this with boiled potatoes and a good dill pickle.

Wiener Roatbraten Steak, Vienna-Style

3   medium onions, sliced thin
4   tablespoons butter
1½ pounds beef sirloin, cut into 3 pieces, ½ inch
    thick, pounded to ¼ inch thick
2   tablespoons butter
    salt
    pepper
1   cup beef stock (use beef bouillon cube)

Sauté the onions in the butter for at least 10 minutes,
till they are crisp. They will burn if you don't watch
them. Stir often, and keep the heat high enough to
brown them without burning them. Remove from
pan; add more butter and the steak, cook 4 to 6 minutes, and season. Remove from pan and add beef
stock; turn the heat all the way up and scrape all the
brown bits from the pan into the stock as it boils.
Pour this onto the steak and add the crisp onions on
top.

Beef Stew with Apples

2   tablespoons oil
2   pounds boneless chuck roast, cut into 4
    pieces
    salt
    pepper
2   cups beef stock (use beef bouillon cubes)
    bay leaf
6   sliced carrots
1   onion, cut into chunks
1   cup applesauce
1   apple, sliced
2   tablespoons cornstarch
½   cup water

Put oil in a heavy casserole, and heat. Add chuck roast, salt, and pepper. Brown the meat on all sides. Add beef stock and bay leaf, bring to boil, turn the heat down, and simmer for 1 hour. Add the carrots, onion, and applesauce. Simmer for another hour. Add the apple; simmer for 15 minutes. Remove the meat, add the cornstarch mixed with the water, simmer, and stir till thick. Return the meat to the pan, and serve.

Swedish Hamburgers

2	tablespoons minced onions
1	tablespoon butter
1	pound ground beef
4	egg yolks
1	tablespoon drained chopped capers
	salt
	pepper
2	teaspoons white vinegar
½	cup cream
¼	cup finely chopped, cooked beets
2–4	tablespoons butter
2	tablespoons oil

Fry the onions in the butter for 5 minutes, remove from pan, and put in bowl. Add to the bowl the ground beef, egg yolks, capers, salt, pepper, vinegar, cream, and beets. Mix and shape into small patties (about 3-4 inches across). Fry in butter and oil about 6 minutes on each side till they're brown. Serve these with fried eggs, if you like.

Burgundy Meatballs

½ pound ground beef
¼ cup breadcrumbs (tear up a slice of bread into
   small pieces)
½ teaspoon onion salt (or ½ teaspoon salt and ¼
   teaspoon onion powder)
¼ teaspoon cornstarch
¼ teaspoon allspice or nutmeg
1 egg, beaten
3 tablespoons oil
½ cup water
¼ cup red wine
2 tablespoons flour
1 beef bouillon cube
   dash of pepper
   rice, potatoes, or noodles

Mix the ground beef, breadcrumbs, onion salt, cornstarch, allspice, and egg. Shape into balls as big as
large walnuts. Brown these in oil; remove from pan.
Add to pan the water, wine, flour, bouillon cube, and
pepper. Blend in pan over moderate heat till smooth.
Add meatballs; boil, cover, and reduce to simmer for
30 minutes. Serve over rice, potatoes, or noodles.

Spiced Flank Steak

2   pounds flank steak
1   onion, chopped
1   bay leaf
2   teaspoons salt
     pepper
3   tablespoons oil
1¼ cup minced onions
1   teaspoon minced garlic
1   cup chopped green pepper
½   teaspoon minced hot pepper
1   large carrot, minced
6   tomatoes (or a 1-pound can, drained),
     minced
⅛   teaspoon cinnamon, ground
⅛   teaspoon cloves, ground
1   teaspoon salt
     pepper
1   tablespoon capers

Boil the flank steak with the onion, bay leaf, salt, and pepper in water to cover it. Lower the heat, and simmer for 1½ hours. Cool the meat and cut it along the grain, about ¼ inch wide. Then cut it in 2-inch pieces. Strain the broth it is cooked in. In the oil, fry the minced onions, garlic, green pepper, hot pepper, and carrot for 5 minutes. Add the tomatoes, cinnamon, cloves, salt, and pepper. Cook on high till liquid is mostly evaporated. Add the meat and 1½ cups of the broth. Add the capers, heat through (about 5 minutes), and serve.

Veal Saltimboca

1	pound veal, thin sliced, pounded to very thin between wax paper
¼	pound cooked ham, thin sliced
	parsley sprigs
	salt
	pepper
½	cup flour
2–4	tablespoons butter
2	tablespoons oil

Cut the veal into palm-size pieces. On each one, lay a slice of ham and two sprigs parsley. Roll the veal up, and pin it with 2 or 3 toothpicks. Mix a little salt and pepper in the flour. Roll each piece of veal in the flour mix and fry till brown in the butter and oil.

Veal with Lemon

	salt
	pepper
¼	cup flour
1	pound veal, thin sliced, pounded to very thin between wax paper
2	tablespoons butter
2	tablespoons oil
½	cup beef stock
6	thin lemon slices
¼	cup more beef stock
1	tablespoon lemon juice
2	tablespoons butter

Mix salt and pepper in the flour, and coat each veal cutlet with the seasoned flour. Brown these in the butter and oil, and remove from pan. Pour off most of the oil remaining in the pan, and add ½ cup beef stock. Boil and scrape the sides and bottom so the brown bits mix with the stock. (This is called deglazing the pan and is usually done with stock or wine.) Return the veal to the pan, and add lemon slices. Cover; simmer for 10 minutes. Remove the meat again, add ¼ cup more beef stock, and deglaze the pan again. Add the lemon juice and the butter. When the butter melts, pour the sauce on the veal and serve.

Baked Fish with Onions and Almonds

½ cup blanched almonds
1 cup minced onions
1 teaspoon minced garlic
1 tablespoon minced parsley
2 tablespoons olive oil
½ cup chicken stock (use chicken bouillon cube)
½ teaspoon salt
4 tablespoons oil
1 large onion, thin sliced
½ teaspoon dried thyme
1 bay leaf, crumbled
½ to 1 pound Haddock, or any firm white
   fleshy fish
¼ cup lime juice
½ teaspoon salt
   pepper
½ cup chicken stock

Toast the almonds in a 350° oven for 10 minutes, then grind them in a blender. Fry them with the onions, garlic, and parsley in the oil for 5 minutes, then add the stock and salt. Stir these together off the heat. Oil a shallow baking pan with the other oil, and spread the bottom with the onion slices. Scatter the thyme and bay leaf over this. Then add the fish, lime juice, salt, pepper, and chicken stock. Spread the fish with the almond-onion paste, and bake uncovered in a 400° oven for 40 minutes.

Salmon Steaks with Herbed Butter

4 tablespoons butter
1 tablespoon minced shallots (or green onions)
1 teaspoon minced garlic
2 tablespoons minced parsley (or oregano, basil, or tarragon)
  salt
  pepper
2 one-inch salmon steaks, each about ¾ pound
  lemon slices

Mix first 6 ingredients, dry the salmon steaks, and brush them with the mixture. Broil the steaks 3 minutes on each side about 3 inches from the heat and baste. Broil another 3 minutes on each side. Baste each time you turn the steaks. Finish cooking by broiling 8 minutes on each side. Spread the remaining butter on the steaks, and serve with the lemon slices.

Danish Hamburgers

1 pound ground meat (it's best if it's half ground pork, but beef will do)
1 onion, pureed (use a blender)
3 tablespoons flour
1 cup club soda
1 egg, well beaten
  salt
  pepper
2 tablespoons butter
2 tablespoons oil

Mix first 7 ingredients together; beat with a fork till fluffy. Cover, and refrigerate for at least 1 hour. Shape mixture into oblongs 4" x 2" x 1". Fry in butter and oil 8 minutes per side till deep brown.

Prawns Mandarin

1   teaspoon root ginger, minced fine (you can use ground ginger, but it doesn't taste the same)

2   teaspoons soy sauce

2   teaspoons sherry

½   pound prawns

2   tablespoons oil

1–2 cups fresh green beans or snow peas or broccoli flowerets or whatever you like

1   tablespoon cornstarch mixed with ½ cup chicken stock or water

Mix the ginger with the soy sauce and sherry, add the prawns, and marinate for 15 minutes. (You must remove the shells from the shrimp. The easiest way is to slit each with a small sharp knife up the belly between the claws and remove the shell. This will take about 15 minutes for ½ pound of shrimp.) Put the oil in a frying pan and heat. When hot, add the shrimp. Do *not* add the marinade. Cook about 5–8 minutes till they turn pink, and then remove them from pan. Add more oil if needed and the vegetables, cut into bite-size pieces. Cook till just tender (about 10 minutes for beans or broccoli, 5 minutes for snow peas), and then add cornstarch and water mixture. Stir quick, and return the shrimp to the pan. Cook about 5–8 minutes, till heated through. Serve with rice.

Shrimp Casalinga

1   clove garlic
1   red-hot pepper
4   tablespoons olive oil
1   pound shrimp, deshelled
2   tablespoons chopped parsley
1   tablespoon capers
    juice of half a lemon
½   teaspoon salt

Cook the garlic and the pepper in the olive oil till they're brown. Remove them, and discard. Add the shrimp, and stir-cook till they're pink. Add the parsley, capers, lemon juice, and salt. Cook for 3 minutes. Serve over rice.

COOKING FROM CANS

Canned soups are great and easy. Mix them, if you like—cream of mushroom with cream of chicken. Make some combinations if you get bored. They mix well with macaroni, too. There are often recipes printed on the can, very easy recipes.

Canned hash, tuna, and salmon can be turned into a meal. Make a tuna casserole, but use salmon instead. Try salmon mixed with mayonnaise and chopped pickle (either sweet or dill) and lettuce for sandwiches. Canned stew is often good. Find a brand that you like.

TV dinners—some folks swear by them, others at them. Try them out. *If all else fails, popcorn is filling!*

SUPPORT GROUPS

BREASTFEEDING HELP OR INFORMATION

La Leche League International
9616 Minneapolis Avenue
Franklin Park, IL 60131
(312) 455-7730

Provides information as well as help with breastfeeding. Check the phone book for the La Leche League group nearest your home. If there is no listing, contact the central office for a referral.

La Leche League also holds monthly meetings, sponsors conferences throughout the country, and publishes many informative pamphlets. Write for more information.

Other Nursing Mothers' Groups. There are numerous groups to help breastfeeding families. Contact your local childbirth educator for information.

CESAREAN BIRTH

Cesareans/Support, Education and Concern (C/SEC)
22 Forest Road
Framingham, MA 01701
(617) 877-8266

Provides information on cesarean prevention, vaginal birth after a cesarean, and emotional support for cesarean families.

The Cesarean Prevention Movement
P.O. Box 152, University Station
Syracuse, NY 13210
(315) 424-1942

Provides information on cesarean prevention and vaginal birth after cesarean and publishes a newsletter, *Cesarean Prevention Clarion.*

SELECTED READING LIST

LABOR AND BIRTH

Sharing Birth: A Father's Guide to Giving Support During Labor, by Carl Jones. (NY: William Morrow, 1985).
"The Labor Support Guide—For Fathers, Family and Friends" (pamphlet), by Carl Jones, Henri Goer, and Penny Simkin. Order from Pennypress, Inc., 1100 Twenty-third Avenue East, Seattle, WA 98112.
Mind Over Labor: Using Mental Imagery to Reduce the Fear and Pain of Labor, by Carl Jones. (NY: Viking/Penguin, 1987).
Deliver Us From Surgery: The Couple's Guide to Cesarean Prevention, by Carl Jones. (NY: Dodd, Mead, 1986).

THE POSTPARTUM PERIOD

After the Baby Is Born, by Carl Jones. (NY: Dodd, Mead, 1986).

Couples With Children, by Randy Meyers Wolfson and Virginia DeLuca. (NY: Dembner, 1981).

Bonding: The Beginnings of Parent-Infant Attachments, by Marshall Klaus and John H. Kennell. (NY: New American Library, 1983).

Premature Babies: Different Beginning, by William A. Sammons and Jennifer Lewis. (St. Louis: C. V. Mosby, 1985).

NURSING

The Womanly Art of Breastfeeding, by La Leche League International. (NY: New American Library, 1981).

Nursing Your Baby, by Karen Pryor. (NY: Pocket Books, 1975).

FATHERHOOD

The Birth of a Father, by Martin Greenberg, M.D. (NY: Continuum, 1985).

Expectant Fathers, by Sam Bittman and Sue Rosenberg Zalk. (NY: Ballantine, 1978).

Fatherhood U.S.A. (Resource Directory), by Debra G. Klinman and Rhiana Kohl. (NY: Garland, 1984).

PREPARING CHILDREN
FOR THE NEWBORN

The New Baby at Your House, by Joanna Cole. (NY: William Morrow, 1985).
Mom and Dad and I Are Having a Baby, by M. Malecky. (Seattle: Pennypress, 1979).

If you can't find any of the above titles in your local bookstore, all of them can be ordered through:

Birth and Life Bookstore
P.O. Box 70625
Seattle, WA 98107

Birth and Life also publishes an informative review of new childbirth-oriented books.

These books can also be ordered through:

NAPSAC Bookstore
P.O. Box 429
Marble Hill, MO 63764

The National Association for Parents and Professionals for Safe Alternatives (NAPSAC) also publishes a newsletter about alternatives in childbirth.

NOTES